♌ LOVE SIGNS ♌

LEO

23 July – 23 August

JULIA & DEREK PARKER

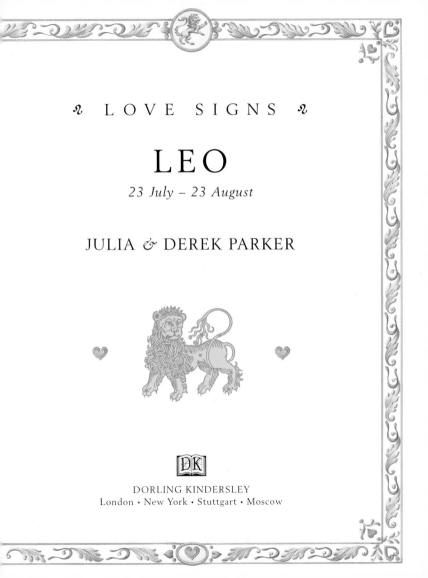

DK

DORLING KINDERSLEY
London • New York • Stuttgart • Moscow

Dedicated to Martin Lethbridge

A DORLING KINDERSLEY BOOK

Project Editor • Annabel Morgan
Art Editor • Anna Benjamin
Managing Editor • Francis Ritter
Managing Art Editor • Derek Coombes
DTP Designer • Cressida Joyce
Production Controller • Martin Croshaw

ACKNOWLEDGMENTS

Photography: Steve Gorton: pp. 10, 13–15, 17–19, 46–49; Ian O'Leary: 16. *Additional photography by:* Colin Keates, Dave King, Monique Le Luhandre, David Murray, Tim Ridley, Clive Streeter, Harry Taylor, Matthew Ward. *Artworks:* Nici Demin: 34–45; Peter Lawman: *jacket*, 4, 12; Paul Redgrave: 24–33; Satwinder Sehmi: *glyphs*; Jane Thomson: *borders*; Rosemary Woods: 11. Peter Lawman's paintings are exhibited by the Portal Gallery Ltd, London.

Picture credits: Bridgeman Art Library/Hermitage, St. Petersburg: 51; Robert Harding Picture Library: 20l, 20c, 20r; Images Colour Library: 9; The National Gallery, London: 11; Tony Stone Images: 21t, 21b; The Victoria and Albert Museum, London: 5; Zefa: 21c.

Thanks to: Sarah Ashun, Emma Brogi, Charlie Chan, John Filbey, Jane Lawrie, Sharon Lucas, Daniel McCarthy, Marion McLornan, Christine Rista, Ola Rudowska, Tim Scott, Isobel Sinden, Martha Swift, Mark Thurgood, Cangy Venables *and* Liz Wagstaff.

First published in Great Britain in 1996 by
Dorling Kindersley Limited, 9 Henrietta Street, London WC2E 8PS

ISBN 0-7513-0330-5

Reproduced by Bright Arts, Hong Kong
Printed and bound by Imago, Hong Kong

CONTENTS

ASTROLOGY & YOU

THERE IS MUCH MORE TO ASTROLOGY THAN YOUR SUN SIGN.
A SIMPLE INVESTIGATION INTO THE POSITION OF THE OTHER
PLANETS AT THE MOMENT OF YOUR BIRTH WILL PROVIDE YOU
WITH FASCINATING INSIGHTS INTO YOUR PERSONALITY.

Your birth sign, or Sun sign, is the sign of the zodiac that the Sun occupied at the moment of your birth. The majority of books on astrology concentrate only on explaining the relevance of the Sun signs. This is a simple form of astrology that can provide you with some interesting but rather general information about you and your personality. In this book, we take you a step further, and reveal how the planets Venus and Mars work in association with your Sun sign to influence your attitudes towards romance and sexuality.

In order to gain a detailed insight into your personality, a "natal" horoscope, or birth chart, is necessary. This details the position of all the planets in our solar system at the moment of your birth, not just the position of the Sun. Just as the Sun occupied one of the 12 zodiac signs when you were born, perhaps making you "a Geminian" or "a Sagittarian", so each of the other planets occupied a certain sign. Each planet governs a different area of your personality, and the planets Venus and Mars are responsible for your attitudes to love and sex respectively.

For example, if you are a Sun-sign Sagittarian, according to the attributes of the sign you should be a dynamic, freedom-loving character. However, if Venus occupied Libra when you were born, you may make rather a passive and clinging partner – qualities that are supposedly completely alien to Sagittarians.

A MAP OF THE CONSTELLATION

The 16th-century astronomer Copernicus first made the revolutionary suggestion that the planets orbit the Sun rather than the Earth. In this 17th-century constellation chart, the Sun is shown at the centre of the solar system.

The tables on pages 52–61 of this book will enable you to discover the positions of Mars and Venus at the moment of your birth. Once you have gleaned this information, turn to pages 22–45. On these pages we explain how the influences of Venus and Mars interact with the characteristics of your Sun sign. This information will provide you with many illuminating insights into your personality, and explains how the planets have formed your attitudes to love and sex.

LOOKING FOR A LOVER

ASTROLOGY CAN PROVIDE YOU WITH VALUABLE INFORMATION
ON HOW TO INITIATE AND MAINTAIN RELATIONSHIPS. IT CAN
ALSO TELL YOU HOW COMPATIBLE YOU ARE WITH YOUR LOVER,
AND HOW SUCCESSFUL YOUR RELATIONSHIP IS LIKELY TO BE.

*P*eople frequently use astrology to lead into a relationship, and "What sign are you?" is often used as a conversation opener. Some people simply introduce the subject as an opening gambit, while others place great importance on this question and its answer.

Astrology can affect the way you think and behave when you are in love. It can also provide you with fascinating information about your lovers and your relationships. Astrology cannot tell you who to fall in love with, or who to avoid, but it can offer you some very helpful advice.

BIRTH CHARTS
Synastry involves the comparison of two people's charts in order to assess their compatibility in all areas of their relationship. The process can highlight any areas of common interest or potential conflict.

People whose signs are grouped under the same element tend to find it easy to fall into a happy relationship. The groupings are:

FIRE: *Aries, Leo, Sagittarius*
EARTH: *Taurus, Virgo, Capricorn*
AIR: *Gemini, Libra, Aquarius*
WATER: *Cancer, Scorpio, Pisces*

When you meet someone to whom you are attracted, astrology can provide you with a valuable insight into his or her personality. It may even reveal unattractive characteristics that your prospective partner is trying to conceal.

Astrologers are often asked to advise lovers involved in an ongoing relationship, or people who are contemplating a love affair. This important aspect of astrology is called synastry, and involves comparing the birth charts of the two people concerned. Each birth chart records the exact position of the planets at the moment and place of a person's birth.

By interpreting each chart separately, then comparing them, an astrologer can assess the compatibility of any two people, showing where problems may arise in their relationship, and where strong bonds will form.

One of the greatest astrological myths is that people of some signs are not compatible with people of certain other signs. This is completely untrue. Whatever your Sun sign, you can have a happy relationship with a person of any other sign.

YOU & YOUR LOVER

KNOWING ABOUT YOURSELF AND YOUR LOVER IS THE KEY TO
A HAPPY RELATIONSHIP. HERE WE REVEAL THE TRADITIONAL
ASSOCIATIONS OF LEO, YOUR COMPATIBILITY WITH ALL THE
SUN SIGNS, AND THE FLOWERS LINKED WITH EACH SIGN.

THE BAY TREE
IS LINKED
WITH LEO

ALL THE
COLOURS
OF THE SUN
ARE LINKED
WITH LEO

GOLD IS THE
LEO METAL

BRIGHT
YELLOW
MARIGOLDS
ARE LEO
FLOWERS

LEOS HAVE
EXCELLENT
POSTURE, AND
ALWAYS STAND
UPRIGHT

THE LEOPARD,
AND OTHER
MEMBERS OF THE
CAT FAMILY,
ARE RULED
BY LEO

VINES AND
WINE ARE
GOVERNED
BY THIS SIGN

LEO AND ARIES

This is a flamboyant and dynamic combination. You are both demanding, and could become competitive. However, this could be one of the most exciting and lively alliances in the zodiac.

Lavender is a Geminian flower

Thistles are ruled by Aries

LEO AND TAURUS

You will bring sparkle and drama to a stolid Taurean, while they will provide you with plenty of attention and support. You are both extremely stubborn, which could cause a few problems.

LEO AND GEMINI

A lively, fun-loving combination. You must not allow Geminian flirtatiousness to worry you – their need for excitement and variety does not mean that they love you any the less.

The lily, and other white flowers, are ruled by Cancer

The rose is associated with Taurus

LEO AND CANCER

Sensitive, loving Cancerians will be happy to provide you with the attention and admiration you crave. However, Cancerians may not be colourful and dramatic enough to hold your interest.

– YOU & YOUR LOVER –

LEO AND LEO

When two warm-hearted Leos get together, they know how to have a good time. However, you may have a little too much in common, both determined to win all the glory and attention.

*Hydrangeas
are governed by Libra*

*Sunflowers
are ruled
by Leo*

LEO AND LIBRA

Tactful and considerate Librans will flatter and compliment you, and in return you will encourage them to be a little more dynamic and active. This has the potential to be a perfect partnership.

*Honeysuckle is
attributed to Scorpio*

LEO AND VIRGO

Modest and self-possessed Virgoans love to serve, and will lavish you with all the attention that you demand. However, you will not take kindly to an excess of Virgoan criticism.

*Small, brightly-coloured flowers
are associated with Virgo*

LEO AND SCORPIO

Scorpio passion and energy matches your own, but is of a very different character. You can expect tempestuous clashes in this relationship – at least life is guaranteed never to be dull.

LEO AND SAGITTARIUS

Two optimistic, warm-hearted fire signs have much in common, and you are capable of forming a carefree and contented alliance. Sagittarian honesty will puncture any Leonine pretensions.

Orchids are associated with Aquarius

Carnations are ruled by Sagittarius

LEO AND AQUARIUS

Cool, independent Aquarians will not respond to your passion and exuberance. You two have little in common, and both must be prepared to work hard to make this alliance succeed.

LEO AND CAPRICORN

You are both ambitious and eager to succeed. Your cheerfulness and optimism will temper Capricornian pessimism, and they will bring you a hint of caution and common sense.

Viburnum is governed by Pisces

Pansies are Capricornian flowers

LEO AND PISCES

Passion, drama, emotion – this will be an affair to remember. Dreamy Pisces will lavish you with attention and emotion, and your warmth and affection will boost their self-confidence.

THE FOOD OF LOVE

WHEN PLANNING A SEDUCTION, THE SENSUOUS DELIGHTS OF AN
EXQUISITE MEAL SHOULD NEVER BE UNDERESTIMATED. READ ON
TO DISCOVER THE PERFECT MEAL FOR EACH OF THE SUN SIGNS,
GUARANTEED TO AROUSE INTEREST AND STIR DESIRE.

*Leos will love
elegant and
sophisticated
dishes such as
pears cooked
in wine.*

- THE FOOD OF LOVE -

FOR ARIENS

Spicy mulligatawny soup

·

Peppered steak

·

Baked Alaska

FOR TAUREANS

Cream of cauliflower soup

·

Tournedos Rossini

·

Rich chocolate and brandy mousse

FOR GEMINIANS

Seafood and avocado salad

·

Piquant stir-fried pork with ginger

·

Zabaglione

FOR CANCERIANS

Artichoke vinaigrette

·

Sole Bonne Femme

·

Almond soufflé

- THE FOOD OF LOVE -

FOR LEOS
Roasted tomato and garlic soup
·
Boeuf Stroganoff
·
Pears cooked in wine

FOR VIRGOANS
Aubergine salad
·
Paella
·
French apple tart

FOR LIBRANS
Asparagus with hollandaise sauce
·
Pork steak with roasted apples
·
Strawberry Pavlova

FOR SCORPIOS
Vichyssoise
·
Lobster Newburg
·
Blackcurrant fool

– THE FOOD OF LOVE –

FOR SAGITTARIANS
Chilled cucumber soup
·
Nutty onion flan
·
Rhubarb crumble with fresh cream

FOR CAPRICORNIANS
Eggs Florentine
·
Pork tenderloin stuffed with sage
·
Pineapple Pavlova

FOR AQUARIANS
Watercress soup
·
Chicken cooked with chilli and lime
·
Lemon soufflé

FOR PISCEANS
French onion soup
·
Trout au vin rosé
·
Melon sorbet

PLACES TO LOVE

ONCE YOU HAVE WON YOUR LOVER'S HEART, A ROMANTIC
HOLIDAY TOGETHER WILL SET THE SEAL ON YOUR LOVE.
HERE YOU CAN DISCOVER THE PERFECT DESTINATION FOR EACH
SUN SIGN, FROM HISTORIC CITIES TO IDYLLIC BEACHES.

THE
EIFFEL
TOWER,
PARIS

ARIES

*Florence is an Arien
city, and its perfectly
preserved Renaissance
palaces and churches
will set the scene for
wonderful romance.*

GEMINI

*Vivacious and restless
Geminians will feel at
home in the fast-paced
and sophisticated
atmosphere of
New York.*

TAURUS

*The unspoilt scenery
and unhurried pace
of life in rural Ireland
is sure to appeal to
patient and placid
Taureans.*

CANCER

*The watery beauty
and uniquely romantic
atmosphere of Venice
is guaranteed to arouse
passion and stir the
Cancerian imagination.*

ST. BASIL'S
CATHEDRAL,
MOSCOW

AYERS ROCK/ULURU,
AUSTRALIA

THE PYRAMIDS,
EGYPT

LEO

*Leos will fall in love
all over again when
surrounded by the
picturesque charm and
unspoilt medieval
atmosphere of Prague.*

SAGITTARIUS

*The wide-ranging
spaces of the Australian
outback will appeal
to the Sagittarian love
of freedom and the
great outdoors.*

GONDOLAS,
VENICE

VIRGO

*Perhaps the most
elegant and romantic
of all cities, Paris is
certainly the ideal
setting for a stylish and
fastidious Virgoan.*

CAPRICORN

*Capricornians will be
fascinated and inspired
by the great historical
monuments of Moscow,
the most powerful of all
Russian cities.*

LIBRA

*The dramatic and
exotic beauty of Upper
Egypt and the Nile will
provide the perfect
backdrop for wooing
a romantic Libran.*

AQUARIUS

*Intrepid Aquarians will
be enthralled and
amazed by the unusual
sights and spectacular
landscapes of the
Indian subcontinent.*

SCORPIO

*Intense and passionate
Scorpios will be strongly
attracted by the whiff
of danger present in
the exotic atmosphere
of New Orleans.*

PISCES

*Water-loving Pisceans
will be at their most
relaxed and romantic
by the sea, perhaps on
a small and unspoilt
Mediterranean island.*

THE TAJ MAHAL,
INDIA

VENUS & MARS

LUCID, SHINING VENUS AND FIERY, RED MARS HAVE ALWAYS BEEN
ASSOCIATED WITH HUMAN LOVE AND PASSION. THE TWO
PLANETS HAVE A POWERFUL INFLUENCE ON OUR ATTITUDES
TOWARDS LOVE, SEX, AND RELATIONSHIPS.

The study of astrology
first began long before
humankind began to record
its own history. The earliest
astrological artefacts discovered,
scratches on bones recording the
phases of the Moon, date from
well before the invention of any
alphabet or writing system.

The planets Venus and Mars
have always been regarded as
having enormous significance
in astrology. This is evident from
the tentative attempts of early
astrologers to record the effects
of the two planets on humankind.
Hundreds of years later, the
positions of the planets were
carefully noted in personal
horoscopes. The earliest known
record is dated 410 BC: "Venus
[was] in the Bull, and Mars in
the Twins".

The bright, shining planet Venus
represents the gentle effect of
the soul on our physical lives.
It is responsible for a refined
and romantic sensuality – "pure"
love, untainted by sex. Venus
reigns over our attitudes towards
romance and the spiritual
dimension of love.

The planet Mars affects the
physical aspects of our lives –
our strength, both physical
and mental; our endurance; and
our ability to fight for survival.
Mars is also strongly linked to
the sex drive of both men and
women. Mars governs our
physical energy, sexuality, and
levels of desire.

Venus is known as an
"inferior" planet, because its
orbit falls between Earth and
the Sun. Venus orbits the Sun

LOVE CONQUERS ALL

In Botticelli's Venus and Mars, *the warlike, fiery energy of Mars, the god of war, has been overcome by the gentle charms of Venus, the goddess of love.*

closely, and its position in the zodiac is always in a sign near that of the Sun. As a result, the planet can only have occupied one of five given signs at the time of your birth – your Sun sign, or the two signs before or after it. For example, if you were born with the Sun in Virgo, Venus can only have occupied Cancer, Leo, Virgo, Libra, or Scorpio at that moment.

Mars, on the other hand, is a "superior" planet. Its orbit lies on the other side of the Earth from the Sun, and therefore the planet may have occupied any of the 12 signs at the moment of your birth.

On the following pages (24–45) we provide you with fascinating insights into how Mars and Venus govern your attitudes towards love, sex, and relationships. To ascertain which sign of the zodiac the planets occupied at the moment of your birth, you must first consult the tables on pages 52–61. Then turn to page 24 and read on.

YOUR LOVE LIFE

THE PLANET VENUS REPRESENTS LOVE, HARMONY, AND UNISON.
WORK OUT WHICH SIGN OF THE ZODIAC VENUS OCCUPIED AT
THE TIME OF YOUR BIRTH (SEE PAGES 52–57), AND READ ON.

VENUS IN GEMINI

*V*enus is in a lively and frivolous mood when it occupies Gemini, and the planet will contribute a sense of light-hearted fun to your love life.

Leos in love tend to be both passionate and idealistic, and they often fling themselves into affairs rashly and unrestrainedly. This impulsiveness may be a recipe for disaster. However, if Venus occupied Gemini at the moment of your birth, you are likely to adopt a rather more sanguine and relaxed attitude to affairs of the heart, and may suffer less heartache as a result.

Due to the influence of Gemini, friendship will be one of the most important elements in your relationship. You possess a lively and agile mind, and

your relationship will not succeed if it is based on mere physical attraction alone – intellectual rapport and shared interests also have an important role to play. You are an excellent communicator, and thrive on lively and stimulating debate and discussion.

The influence of Gemini may incline you to be more flirtatious and coquettish than the majority of Leos. Geminis are attracted by variety and novelty, and Venus may bring you a longing for excitement and change. You have a great zest for life and your partner must be as lively and enthusiastic as you if your relationship is to thrive. If a love affair loses its sparkle and lapses into an

entirely predictable routine, you may soon look around for someone new and more exciting.

Due to the vivacious, lively Geminian influence, your natural Leonine exuberance is likely to be increased. You are in your element in a social situation, and solitude and quiet contemplation do not appeal to you in the slightest. Your lover may find your reluctance to spend quiet evenings together insulting, but hopefully will understand that your love of socializing does not lessen your love for him or her.

One final word of warning – Leos can be rather authoritative and autocratic. You may firmly believe that you always know the best way to do everything, and have a talent for giving instructions. Try not to become domineering towards your lover or your relationship may become extremely unbalanced.

VENUS IN CANCER

*L*eos born when Venus shines from Cancer will be emotional, romantic, and sensitive.

Venus from Cancer will make you an extremely adoring and affectionate lover. You have a strong nurturing instinct, and will pamper and cherish your lover in a delightful fashion. However, do not allow yourself to become over-protective and clinging towards your partner, who could begin to feel confined and restricted. You must make sure that you do not adopt a parental role towards your lover, as this is not exactly conducive to passion and romance.

You will be very idealistic, and need to look up to your partner. When you fall in love, you have a dangerous tendency to place your lover on a pedestal and adulate him or her; then, if any faults are revealed, as they inevitably will, you will feel hurt and disillusioned.

Do not force your lover to live up to your high expectations – it is unfair to both of you.

Due to the combined influences of Cancer and Leo, you are likely to be very warm and affectionate. You may also find that you are extremely sentimental and sensitive. Both Cancerians and Leos are easily hurt, and a thoughtless word or action can cut you to the quick. Due to the influence of Cancer, you can be moody, and if you are feeling discontented or disappointed your tongue may be very sharp and scathing. Try not to take out your frustrations on your friends or family. Luckily, you are likely to possess plenty of Leonine cheerfulness and resilience, and your optimism will soon lift you out of any bad moods.

Your tendency to be slightly dictatorial and overbearing will be mitigated by the soothing and

sympathetic influence of Venus
in Cancer. Instead, you will use
your intuition and shrewdness to
ensure you get your own way.

As a Sun-sign Leo, you have
a propensity to over-dramatize
a situation, but you must try
to control this habit, because
constant scenes and melodramas
will eventually prove irritating
and exhausting for your partner.
Resist the temptation to indulge
in histrionics, and concentrate

instead on expressing your
powerful emotional forces
honestly and positively.

Due to the influence of
Cancer, your emotions are likely
to be volatile and mercurial and
therefore domestic stability will
play an important role in your
life. You will focus much of
your time and energy on the
home that you create with your
partner, and it will represent
a real haven to you.

VENUS IN LEO

*W*hen Venus shares the sign of Leo with the Sun, all the classic Leo qualities are emphasized and enhanced.

You are outgoing, exuberant, and warm-hearted, and should have no problem attracting prospective lovers. When you fall in love, you will initially regard your lover as the absolute epitome of perfection, and will be immensely proud of his or her achievements. You will prove a source of endless encouragement, urging your partner on to fresh achievements. Do not unwittingly put your lover under great pressure to succeed, because if your demands are excessive, you may find that your partner begins to resent you.

You may also have to struggle against the temptation to try and run your lover's life. Leos have a worrying tendency to dominate their partners, and when the Sun and Venus both occupy Leo, this quality may be heightened. Do not allow it to get out of control – repress your inclination towards bossiness and instead employ the arts of tact and diplomacy.

You will be an ardent and exciting lover, and will lavish an abundance of affection and attention on your partner. Your fiery and passionate emotions will be expressed openly and unashamedly, and sometimes in such a dramatic fashion that you and your lover become the centre of attention. A more modest and reserved personality may not feel comfortable with your fulsome compliments or boisterous physical expressions of emotion. They may even find your attentions embarassing and excessive. Try to understand that not everyone thrives on drama and excitement, and that your exuberance and theatricality may frighten off prospective partners.

Leo rules the heart, and you are likely to be extremely generous both financially and emotionally. You enjoy luxury, and will wine and dine your prospective partners in the most lavish and elegant surroundings possible.

Friendship is very important and meaningful to a Leo, and it takes time before you consider someone a true friend. Once you have become close to someone, you are extremely faithful and loyal. You are a good listener, and your friends will instinctively turn to you in their hour of need, knowing you will provide them with a shoulder to cry on and some helpful and honest advice. Make sure that you do not become too domineering, and avoid telling your friends what they should do and how to do it. Remember that there is a very fine line between helpful advice and bossy instructions.

VENUS IN VIRGO

For Sun-sign Leos, the placing of Venus in Virgo can prove extremely positive and beneficial. It will encourage you to be more selective and judicious when choosing a lover, rather than falling head over heels in love with the first likely candidate, as many Leos do.

Although the influence of Virgo may make you slightly more sensible and restrained, the Virgoan yearning for perfection may manifest itself in your personality, and combine with the innate romanticism of the Leo. Behind a practical and rational exterior, you are likely to be an incurable romantic, with a head full of idealistic dreams of chivalry and perfect love.

The Virgoan influence may cause you to adopt a critical attitude towards those you love, while Leos can often assume a rather domineering position within a relationship. Make

sure that you do not become too exacting or deprecating towards your partner. Much to your surprise, you may discover that most people do not enjoy having their faults constantly pointed out to them, and your critical attitude may do damage to an otherwise perfect alliance. Try to make sure that your criticisms are constructive and offered in a tactful manner.

The Virgoan influence may encourage you to over-analyze your feelings, and this may inhibit the spontaneous expression of your emotions, making you appear more cool and reserved than many of your fellow Leos. Virgo will not be able to dampen down your Leonine exuberance, but it may subdue it slightly. As a result, you are unlikely to indulge in the dramatic scenes with your partner that so many Leos enjoy. This is not because you are less

loving and passionate than other Leos, merely because you do not thrive on drama and sensation.

There may be a streak of moodiness in your personality, and as a result, your relationship may experience a few emotional upheavals. You may not be very demonstrative, but you should be a good communicator, able to put your feelings into words, and explain to your lover exactly what is upsetting you.

You will not consider someone a friend until he or she has earned your respect and trust. This might take some time, but once you have become close to someone, you are a loyal and faithful friend. The same can be said of your romantic relationships. You may be cautious at first, but once you have committed yourself, you will prove an extremely constant, loving, and supportive partner.

VENUS IN LIBRA

*T*he basic Libran need is to relate to another human being, and when Venus occupies Libra, you may feel that you cannot achieve true harmony and fulfilment in your life without the companionship and love of a long-term partner.

The combination of this yearning for a serious relationship and your Leonine hot-headedness can be a recipe for disaster. You may be so eager for a long-term commitment that you throw caution to the wind, and fling yourself into a love affair with alarming swiftness. This impetuosity is likely to lead to disillusionment, because you may soon discover that you are not as compatible with your lover as you had expected. Try to learn some restraint – it may prevent considerable heartache.

The languid influence of Libra means that you will be more relaxed than many of your fellow Leos. You will be inclined to opt for a quiet life, and may go out of your way to avoid disagreements and confrontations, rather than asserting yourself with all the usual Leo passion and confidence. However, this fear of conflict will not apply to your romantic relationships. Here, you may find that you tend deliberately to provoke your partner and cause arguments simply because you so enjoy kissing and making up afterwards. Try to resist the temptation to create scenes, because you may find that they cause more serious damage to your relationship than you ever anticipated.

Due to the influence of Venus from Libra, you will have an innate appreciation of fine and beautiful objects. Gracious living is very important to you, and you will want to woo your lover in the most luxurious and

elegant of surroundings. You are very generous, both emotionally and financially, and the prospect of scrimping and saving will not appeal in the slightest. Try not to become too extravagant, otherwise you may find yourself living far beyond your means.

Due to the gentle Libran influence, you will be kind, supportive, and understanding, more than willing to listen to your lover's problems and to talk them through. The tactful and tolerant tenderness that Venus brings from Libra will join with the solid and reliable qualities of Leo, making you an extremely loyal and loving friend.

When Venus shines from Libra, the planet emphasizes the most delightful characteristics of the Leo in love, making you romantic and affectionate – both ingredients for a happy and successful relationship.

YOUR SEX LIFE

THE PLANET MARS REPRESENTS PHYSICAL AND SEXUAL ENERGY.
WORK OUT WHICH SIGN OF THE ZODIAC MARS OCCUPIED AT THE
MOMENT OF YOUR BIRTH (SEE PAGES 58–61), AND READ ON.

MARS IN ARIES

*W*hen Mars is in Aries, its energy, assertiveness, and emphasis on the sex drive will heighten your libido and enhance your warm Leonine response to your partner.

Your wholehearted delight and enthusiasm for sex will charm your lovers, and bring an atmosphere of affectionate fun to your lovemaking. However, the passion brought to you by Aries may overwhelm your lovers with its fiery intensity.

If you are unable to satisfy your powerful physical appetite, you may become frustrated and irritable. Remember that plenty of strenuous exercise will help to burn off any excess energy.

MARS IN TAURUS

From Taurus, Mars can increase both your sex drive and the warm sensuality you show your lovers. However, the planet may also incline you to be unusually possessive.

You need an active and uncomplicated sex life, because you are a warmly affectionate lover and need to express your earthy and generous sexuality.

A large portion of Taurean patience will make you calm and placid, but once your temper is roused it may be difficult for you to keep it under control. Try not to express your anger in an aggressive fashion.

Mars will bring you tenacity and determination from Taurus, and due to these qualities you will be able to complete any tasks quickly and thoroughly. However, your increased determination is not always beneficial – it can also make you very stubborn. Even when you are convinced that you are in the right, try to listen to the opinions of your partner.

MARS IN GEMINI

Leos tend to fall in love quickly and passionately, and Mars will not be able to offer you any help from Gemini. You will fling yourself into affairs impulsively and expect your relationships to develop quickly.

Although Leos are sensual and warm partners, they do not usually possess a very highly charged sex drive. However, Mars will manage to boost your sexuality, even though Gemini is a fairly cool sign. Your attitude to sex is light-hearted and

entirely uncomplicated – you are a lively and energetic lover, always eager to experiment. Your affair may not be steamy and intense, but it will certainly be entertaining and fun.

Once involved in a long-term relationship, you will work hard to keep it entertaining and diverting. You revel in admiration and attention, and flirting could become an enjoyable pastime. Your partner may not appreciate this tendency, especially if he or she is of a jealous disposition.

MARS IN CANCER

*W*hen Mars is placed in Cancer, the potent energy of the planet will be expressed emotionally. Your sex life will also be powerfully influenced by the planet, and you will be a caring and sensuous lover, instinctively aware of your lover's desires, and eager to satisfy them.

Due to the influence of Cancer, you may be sensitive and moody. As a result, outbursts of anger will not be unusual. In the heat of an argument, you may not be able to stop yourself from making hurtful comments that would be far better left unsaid. You know exactly how to hit sensitive spots, and your words are guaranteed to sting.

You will be a protective and caring lover, but you must try not to become too clinging. When Mars is in Cancer there is a danger that a claustrophobic atmosphere may pervade your relationship. Try to subdue this tendency, or you may end up driving your partner away, rather than binding him or her to you.

MARS IN LEO

When Mars and the Sun both occupy Leo, they bring energy, enthusiasm, and initiative. You will be a natural leader, with plenty of charisma and excellent organizational skills.

You revel in your warm and sensual Leonine sexuality, and your lovemaking will be both passionate and rewarding. Setting the scene for seduction is important to you, and you will go to great lengths to create an inviting and romantic atmosphere in which to ravish your lover.

Those born with both the Sun and Mars in Leo can have an overbearing manner, and you may find that you have a tendency to dominate others, particularly if they are quieter or less assertive than you. Try not to become too high-handed or domineering towards your partner.

You revel in excitement and drama, and may become an attention seeker. You must try to control the urge to show off, otherwise you may begin to irritate and exhaust your lovers.

MARS IN VIRGO

From Virgo, Mars will bring a very discerning and analytical influence. The more hot-headed and impetuous elements of your personality will be subdued, and you will possess a more sensible and cautious attitude to life. However, do not allow Virgoan discrimination to quash your Leonine enthusiasm.

As far as sex is concerned, quality, not quantity, is the relevant word for a Leo with Mars in Virgo. You are a sensuous and generous lover, but you may find it difficult to express your sexuality – Virgoan modesty and shyness could inhibit you. Try not to repress the voluptuous instincts that Mars can awaken in a sensual earth sign.

Virgo is a particularly hard-working and dutiful sign, and you may find it difficult to relax, suffering pangs of guilt if you put your feet up for a few minutes or have a lie-in. Tell yourself that relaxation is a lesson you must learn, and you may find it easier to unwind.

MARS IN LIBRA

The softening influence of Libra can dilute your Leonine energy, and you may make excuses to avoid strenuous sexual activity. Due to the Libran influence, you may be somewhat languid and lethargic, and the prospect of an energetic night of passion may not instantly appeal. However, once you are aroused, your warm sexuality will be enhanced by Mars in Libra. When you do summon up the energy to make love, you will perform ardently and enthusiastically.

Due to the influence of Libra, you are likely to be a great romantic, with a tendency to fall in love at first sight. Try not to rush into affairs without consideration – due to your idealistic streak, you will be disillusioned and disappointed if your affair fails.

If you allow Mars to stimulate the subtle elements of Libran sexuality rather than weakening them, the softer, more gentle qualities the planet will bring to your personality can only increase your personal attraction.

MARS IN SCORPIO

When the potent energy of Scorpio is brought to bear on a spirited and dynamic Leo personality, sparks may fly.

When Mars occupies this powerful water sign, the planet will greatly increase your Leonine sexual vigour. This is a truly positive attribute, and you must make sure that you express your sexual energy in a rewarding and satisfying way, because the failure to channel your powerful desires in a positive direction may lead to frustration.

Both Leo and Scorpio are highly emotional signs, and you will be a very passionate and adoring lover. However, your relationship is guaranteed to have its fair share of stormy scenes and dramatic arguments.

Jealousy is not a typical Leo trait, but it may present a problem when Mars occupies Scorpio. If you enlist the help of your cheerful and optimistic Leonine disposition, you should be able to counter this irrational and unattractive emotion.

MARS IN SAGITTARIUS

*T*his planetary position gives a great boost to your energy, and you will need a lively partner who can help you burn up some of your boundless physical resources.

Due to the influence of Sagittarius, you may be restless and impatient, eagerly seeking novelty and excitement. You tend to be easily bored, and if your relationship becomes predictable or routine, you may indulge in illicit liaisons or even desert your lover for someone else.

Leos are usually rather conventional types, but this placing of Mars can encourage unexpected and outrageous behaviour. You may set out to purposely shock or tease people who are more conventional and narrow-minded than you are. If your partner is very conformist, your quirky behaviour might prove to be embarrassing.

If you can find a partner who can stimulate your mind and match your physical energy, you should make a perfect match.

MARS IN CAPRICORN

*W*hen Mars shines from Capricorn, you will channel your boundless Leonine energy into hard work and advancement. You will strive to be the best in every activity in which you take part.

In love, as in any other contest, you will be determined to win the first prize. You are extremely forceful, and anyone on whom you set your sights may as well surrender to you immediately. Once involved in a permanent relationship, you are a constant, devoted, and witty lover. Do not allow your ambitions to appropriate too much of your time, or your partner may end up playing second fiddle to your career.

Due to the influence of Mars in Capricorn, you will be an earthy and uncomplicated lover with a strong sex drive. Although you can be cautious when it comes to initiating sexual relationships, once you have committed yourself you are an ardent and passionate lover.

MARS IN AQUARIUS

From Aquarius, Mars will not increase your emotional expression of love, and the planet may even cool your ardour. Although you are not passionate, you greatly enjoy sex and revel in experimentation. Mars will also increase your Leonine desire to ensure that your partners are satisfied and fulfilled within your relationship.

Mars from Aquarius may add an eccentric and unconventional streak to your personality. The influence of Aquarius is unusual and original, and you will be a charmingly unpredictable lover. The Aquarian influence can also indicate a degree of wilfulness, but this is unlikely to become troublesome in a Leo.

Mars in Aquarius encourages independence and detachment. As a result, you may feel reluctant to make a permanent commitment. Hopefully, the warm-hearted influence of Leo will overcome this tendency, because you have much to offer as a long-term partner.

MARS IN PISCES

*M*ars brings a sensual and passionate influence from Pisces. The planet will raise your emotional temperature, and you will be an intensely romantic and poetic lover.

If your fervent emotions are concealed or repressed, there is a danger that you may become discontented and introspective. However, your Leonine openness and honesty will prove invaluable in this respect, and your intense and passionate emotions will flow out in a veritable torrent.

Sex plays an important part in your relationships, and your lovemaking will be skilled, erotic, and imaginative. Both Leo and Pisces are generous and considerate signs, and you will be eager to ensure that your lover is sexually fulfilled and contented.

Remember that a successful relationship requires a solid basis of companionship, as well as physical attraction. Sex is only one element of a relationship, and you must find a lover who will also be your best friend.

TOKENS OF LOVE

ASTROLOGY CAN GIVE YOU A FASCINATING INSIGHT INTO
YOUR LOVER'S PERSONALITY AND ATTITUDE TO LOVE. IT CAN
ALSO PROVIDE YOU WITH SOME INVALUABLE HINTS WHEN YOU
WANT TO CHOOSE THE PERFECT GIFT FOR YOUR LOVER.

ARIES

*The head is the part
of the body ruled by
Aries, therefore a
colourful woolly hat
or some unusual hair
accessories will be
greatly appreciated.*

INDIAN HAIR
ORNAMENT

KNITTED
PERUVIAN
HAT

TAURUS

*Fine, hand-painted
porcelain will
appeal to your
Taurean lover, as
will hand-made
chocolates.*

LIMOGES
PORCELAIN
PILLBOX

GEMINI

*Exotic nuts or a
handsome box of
sugared almonds
will be greatly
appreciated by a
Geminian lover.*

BELGIAN
CHOCOLATES

MACADAMIA
NUTS

HAND-PAINTED
ENAMELLED
PILLBOX WITH
SUN MOTIF

CANCER

*The Cancerian
connection with
water makes an
antique print
of a ship or the
ocean a perfect
present.*

GOLD CROWN
CANDLEHOLDER

LEO

*Gold or gold-
coloured gifts, or
any objects with
a Sun motif, will
delight your Leo lover.*

GOLD
KEY-RING

19TH-CENTURY
PRINT OF A SHIP

GOLD CHAIN
NECKLACE
WITH
HEARTS

WILDFLOWER
HONEY

VIRGO

*Small and dainty pieces
of jewellery will appeal
to your Virgoan lover.
Instead of choosing
chocolates, give a health-
conscious Virgoan a pot
of exotic honey.*

– TOKENS OF LOVE –

**EXPENSIVE
LIPSTICK**

'FRENCH
LACE'
ROSE

LIBRA

*Expensive toiletries will appeal
to a luxury-loving Libran. An
extravagantly large bouquet of
white roses is also guaranteed
to satisfy their
opulent tastes.*

SCORPIO

*Exotic bath
products will
delight your
Scorpio lover,
because Scorpio
is a water sign.
A leather belt
will also please.*

SCENTED
BATH OIL

PATTERNED
LEATHER
BELT

VICTORIAN
TRAVEL
BOOKS

SAGITTARIUS

*Adventurous Sagittarians
love to travel, therefore travel
books and accessories, such
as maps or compasses, will
be greatly appreciated by
a Sagittarian lover.*

ANTIQUE
GLASS
DECANTER

CAPRICORN

*Chunky, simply-
decorated glassware
or a good-quality
antique silver picture
frame will impress
your fastidious
Capricornian lover.*

SILVER
PICTURE
FRAME

GIVING A BIRTHSTONE

*The most personal
gift you can give
your lover is the
gem linked to his
or her Sun sign.*

RUBY

ARIES: *diamond*
TAURUS: *emerald*
GEMINI: *agate* • CANCER: *pearl*
LEO: *ruby* • VIRGO: *sardonyx*
LIBRA: *sapphire* • SCORPIO: *opal*
SAGITTARIUS: *topaz*
CAPRICORN: *amethyst*
AQUARIUS: *aquamarine*
PISCES: *moonstone*

AQUARIUS

*If you want to
give an Aquarian
flowers, choose
orchids. Any
unusual gifts will
be gratefully
received.*

WHITE
ORCHID

PISCES

*Pisceans will appreciate
a soft silk scarf, or a
decorative piece
of mother-
of-pearl.*

SILK
SCARF

MOTHER-
OF-PEARL

YOUR PERMANENT RELATIONSHIP

LEOS MAKE ENERGETIC AND ENTHUSIASTIC PARTNERS, BUT
CAN BE OVERBEARING. IF YOU DOMINATE YOUR PARTNER,
THE EQUILIBRIUM IN YOUR RELATIONSHIP WILL BE UPSET.

*L*eos are particularly eager to have their permanent partnerships formalized by a proper contract. They tend to find informal arrangements a trifle too casual and unofficial.

Leos may appear to have some unconventional attitudes, but at heart they like to feel that they are part of a tradition. If you are a typical Leo, you will want a formal wedding with all the trimmings – top hats, champagne, speeches, and every other imaginable convention. Even if circumstances make this impossible, you will want some kind of celebration of your permanent relationship.

Enjoyment and amusement are important to you, and you will be eager to have plenty of fun with your lover. Leos are always entertaining company, and no lover of yours is likely to complain of boredom.

However short of money you are, you will lavish what little you do have on simple fun. If straitened circumstances mean that an occasion can only be enjoyed over an inexpensive plate of pasta and glass of wine, it will nevertheless be a celebration, and your exuberant, positive attitude will make it just as enjoyable as something more elaborate and extravagant.

Leos are prepared to devote much time and determination to making their partnerships succeed. Your abundance of energy is admirable, but do not become dictatorial. Try to see

On a Sailing Ship, *by Caspar David Friedrich, shows a newly-married couple sailing into a bright but unknown future together.*

things from your partner's point of view, as well as your own, and remember that you can be slightly domineering.

Always having your own way is not good for a dictatorial Leo – try to maintain the equilibrium in your relationship and to occasionally give way graciously, even if your partner is less forceful and assertive than you are. Allow your partner the opportunity to voice his or her opinion and to argue for it. You could be surprised – he or she may even have something worthwhile to contribute.

Leos can put their lovers on a pedestal before discovering that their idols have feet of clay. Expect too much of your lover and you may be disappointed. Try not to be too idealistic, because any heartbreak will take time to heal.

VENUS & MARS TABLES

THESE TABLES WILL ENABLE YOU TO DISCOVER WHICH SIGNS
VENUS AND MARS OCCUPIED AT THE MOMENT OF YOUR BIRTH.
TURN TO PAGES 24–45 TO INVESTIGATE THE QUALITIES OF THESE
SIGNS, AND TO FIND OUT HOW THEY WORK WITH YOUR SUN SIGN.

*T*he tables on pages 53–61 will enable you to discover the positions of Venus and Mars at the moment of your birth.

First find your year of birth on the top line of the appropriate table, then find your month of birth in the left-hand column. Where the column for your year of birth intersects with the row for your month of birth, you will find a group of figures and zodiacal glyphs. These figures and glyphs show which sign of the zodiac the planet occupied

on the first day of that month, and any date during that month on which the planet moved into another sign.

For example, to ascertain the position of Venus on May 10 1968, run your finger down the column marked 1968 until you reach the row for May. The row of numbers and glyphs shows that Venus occupied Aries on May 1, entered Taurus on May 4, and then moved into Gemini on May 28. Therefore, on May 10, Venus was in Taurus.

If you were born on a day when one of the planets was moving into a new sign, it may be impossible to determine your Venus and Mars signs completely accurately. If the characteristics described on the relevant pages do not seem to apply to you, read the interpretation of the sign before and after. One of these signs will be appropriate.

ZODIACAL GLYPHS

♈	Aries	♎	Libra
♉	Taurus	♏	Scorpio
♊	Gemini	♐	Sagittarius
♋	Cancer	♑	Capricorn
♌	Leo	♒	Aquarius
♍	Virgo	♓	Pisces

♀	1921	1922	1923	1924	1925	1926	1927	1928
JAN	1 ♒ 7 ♓	1 ♑ 25 ♒	1 ♏ 14 ♐	1 ♒ 20 ♓	1 ♐ 15 ♑	1 ♒	1 ♑ 10 ♒	1 ♏ 5 ♐ 30 ♑
FEB	1 ♓ 3 ♈	1 ♒ 18 ♓	1 ♐ 7 ♑	1 ♓ 14 ♈	1 ♑ 8 ♒	1 ♒	1 ♒ 3 ♓ 27 ♈	1 ♑ 23 ♒
MAR	1 ♈ 8 ♉	1 ♓ 14 ♈	1 ♑ 7 ♒	1 ♈ 10 ♉	1 ♒ 5 ♓ 29 ♈	1 ♒	1 ♈ 23 ♉	1 ♒ 19 ♓
APR	1 ♉ 26 ♈	1 ♈ 7 ♉	1 ♒ 2 ♓ 27 ♈	1 ♉ 6 ♊	1 ♈ 22 ♉	1 ♒ 7 ♓	1 ♉ 17 ♊	1 ♓ 12 ♈
MAY	1 ♈	1 ♉ 2 ♊ 26 ♋	1 ♈ 22 ♉	1 ♊ 7 ♋	1 ♉ 16 ♊	1 ♓ 2 ♈ 27 ♉	1 ♊ 13 ♋	1 ♈ 7 ♉ 31 ♊
JUN	1 ♈ 3 ♉	1 ♋ 20 ♌	1 ♉ 16 ♊	1 ♋	1 ♊ 10 ♋	1 ♉ 21 ♊	1 ♋ 9 ♌	1 ♊ 24 ♋
JUL	1 ♉ 9 ♊	1 ♌ 16 ♍	1 ♊ 11 ♋	1 ♋	1 ♋ 4 ♌ 29 ♍	1 ♊ 16 ♋	1 ♌ 8 ♍	1 ♋ 19 ♌
AUG	1 ♊ 6 ♋	1 ♍ 11 ♎	1 ♋ 4 ♌ 28 ♍	1 ♋	1 ♍ 23 ♎	1 ♋ 10 ♌	1 ♍	1 ♌ 12 ♍
SEP	1 ♌ 27 ♍	1 ♎ 8 ♏	1 ♍ 22 ♎	1 ♋ 8 ♌	1 ♎ 17 ♏	1 ♌ 4 ♍ 29 ♎	1 ♍	1 ♍ 5 ♎ 30 ♏
OCT	1 ♍ 21 ♎	1 ♏ 11 ♐	1 ♎ 16 ♏	1 ♌ 8 ♍	1 ♏ 8 ♐	1 ♎ 24 ♏	1 ♍	1 ♏ 24 ♐
NOV	1 ♎ 14 ♏	1 ♐ 29 ♏	1 ♏ 9 ♐	1 ♍ 3 ♎ 28 ♏	1 ♐ 7 ♑	1 ♏ 18 ♐	1 ♍ 10 ♎	1 ♐ 18 ♑
DEC	1 ♏ 8 ♐	1 ♏	1 ♐ 3 ♑ 27 ♒	1 ♏ 22 ♐	1 ♑ 6 ♒	1 ♐ 13 ♑	1 ♎ 9 ♏	1 ♑ 13 ♒

♀	1929	1930	1931	1932	1933	1934	1935	1936
JAN	1 ♒ 7 ♓	1 ♑ 25 ♒	1 ♏ 4 ♐	1 ♒ 20 ♓	1 ♐ 15 ♑	1 ♒	1 ♑ 9 ♒	1 ♏ 4 ♐ 29 ♑
FEB	1 ♓ 3 ♈	1 ♒ 17 ♓	1 ♐ 7 ♑	1 ♓ 13 ♈	1 ♑ 8 ♒	1 ♒	1 ♒ 2 ♓ 27 ♈	1 ♑ 23 ♒
MAR	1 ♈ 9 ♉	1 ♓ 13 ♈	1 ♑ 6 ♒	1 ♈ 10 ♉	1 ♒ 4 ♓ 28 ♈	1 ♒	1 ♈ 23 ♉	1 ♒ 18 ♓
APR	1 ♉ 21 ♈	1 ♈ 7 ♉	1 ♒ 1 ♓ 26 ♈	1 ♉ 6 ♊	1 ♈ 21 ♉	1 ♒ 7 ♓	1 ♉ 17 ♊	1 ♓ 12 ♈
MAY	1 ♈	1 ♊ 26 ♋	1 ♈ 21 ♉	1 ♊ 7 ♋	1 ♉ 16 ♊	1 ♓ 2 ♈ 27 ♉	1 ♊ 12 ♋	1 ♈ 6 ♉ 30 ♊
JUN	1 ♈ 4 ♉	1 ♋ 20 ♌	1 ♉ 15 ♊	1 ♋	1 ♊ 9 ♋	1 ♉ 21 ♊	1 ♋ 8 ♌	1 ♊ 24 ♋
JUL	1 ♉ 9 ♊	1 ♌ 15 ♍	1 ♊ 10 ♋	1 ♋ 14 ♊ 29 ♋	1 ♋ 4 ♌ 28 ♍	1 ♊ 16 ♋	1 ♌ 8 ♍	1 ♋ 18 ♌
AUG	1 ♊ 6 ♋	1 ♍ 11 ♎	1 ♋ 4 ♌ 28 ♍	1 ♋	1 ♍ 22 ♎	1 ♋ 10 ♌	1 ♍	1 ♌ 12 ♍
SEP	1 ♌ 26 ♍	1 ♎ 8 ♏	1 ♍ 21 ♎	1 ♋ 9 ♌	1 ♎ 16 ♏	1 ♌ 4 ♍ 29 ♎	1 ♍	1 ♍ 5 ♎ 29 ♏
OCT	1 ♍ 21 ♎	1 ♏ 11 ♐	1 ♎ 15 ♏	1 ♌ 8 ♍	1 ♏ 8 ♐	1 ♎ 24 ♏	1 ♍	1 ♏ 24 ♐
NOV	1 ♎ 14 ♏	1 ♐ 23 ♏	1 ♏ 8 ♐	1 ♍ 3 ♎ 28 ♏	1 ♐ 7 ♑	1 ♏ 23 ♐	1 ♍ 10 ♎	1 ♐ 17 ♑
DEC	1 ♏ 8 ♐ 31 ♑	1 ♏	1 ♐ 2 ♑ 26 ♒	1 ♏ 22 ♐	1 ♑ 6 ♒	1 ♐ 17 ♑	1 ♎ 9 ♏	1 ♑ 12 ♒

♀	1937	1938	1939	1940	1941	1942	1943	1944
JAN	1 ♒ · 7 ♓	1 ♑ · 24 ♒	1 ♏ · 5 ♐	1 ♒ · 19 ♓	1 ♐ · 14 ♑	1 ♒	1 ♑ · 9 ♒	1 ♏ · 4 ♐ · 29 ♑
FEB	1 ♓ · 3 ♈	1 ♒ · 17 ♓	1 ♐ · 7 ♑	1 ♓ · 13 ♈	1 ♑ · 7 ♒	1 ♒	1 ♒ · 2 ♓ · 26 ♈	1 ♑ · 22 ♒
MAR	1 ♈ · 10 ♉	1 ♓ · 13 ♈	1 ♑ · 6 ♒	1 ♈ · 9 ♉	1 ♒ · 3 ♓ · 28 ♈	1 ♒	1 ♈ · 22 ♉	1 ♒ · 18 ♓
APR	1 ♉ · 15 ♈	1 ♈ · 6 ♉ · 30 ♊	1 ♓ · 26 ♈	1 ♉ · 5 ♊	1 ♈ · 21 ♉	1 ♒ · 7 ♓	1 ♉ · 16 ♊	1 ♓ · 11 ♈
MAY	1 ♈	1 ♊ · 25 ♋	1 ♈ · 21 ♉	1 ♊ · 19 ♋	1 ♉ · 15 ♊	1 ♓ · 6 ♈	1 ♊ · 12 ♋	1 ♈ · 5 ♉ · 30 ♊
JUN	1 ♈ · 5 ♉	1 ♋ · 19 ♌	1 ♉ · 15 ♊	1 ♋ · 28 ♊	1 ♊ · 8 ♋	1 ♈ · 3 ♉ · 28 ♊	1 ♋ · 8 ♌	1 ♊ · 23 ♋
JUL	1 ♉ · 8 ♊	1 ♌ · 15 ♍	1 ♊ · 10 ♋	1 ♊	1 ♋ · 3 ♌ · 28 ♍	1 ♊ · 24 ♋	1 ♌ · 8 ♍	1 ♋ · 18 ♌
AUG	1 ♊ · 3 ♋	1 ♍ · 10 ♎	1 ♋ · 3 ♌ · 27 ♍	1 ♊ · 2 ♋	1 ♍ · 22 ♎	1 ♋ · 18 ♌	1 ♍	1 ♌ · 11 ♍
SEP	1 ♌ · 26 ♍	1 ♎ · 8 ♏	1 ♍ · 21 ♎	1 ♋ · 9 ♌	1 ♎ · 16 ♏	1 ♌ · 11 ♍	1 ♍	1 ♍ · 4 ♎ · 29 ♏
OCT	1 ♍ · 20 ♎	1 ♏ · 14 ♐	1 ♎ · 15 ♏	1 ♌ · 15 ♍	1 ♏ · 11 ♐	1 ♍ · 5 ♎ · 29 ♏	1 ♍	1 ♏ · 23 ♐
NOV	1 ♎ · 13 ♏	1 ♐ · 16 ♏	1 ♏ · 8 ♐	1 ♍ · 2 ♎ · 27 ♏	1 ♐ · 7 ♑	1 ♏ · 22 ♐	1 ♍ · 10 ♎	1 ♐ · 17 ♑
DEC	1 ♏ · 7 ♐ · 31 ♑	1 ♏	1 ♐ · 2 ♑ · 26 ♒	1 ♏ · 21 ♐	1 ♑ · 6 ♒	1 ♐ · 16 ♑	1 ♎ · 9 ♏	1 ♑ · 12 ♒

♀	1945	1946	1947	1948	1949	1950	1951	1952
JAN	1 ♒ · 6 ♓	1 ♑ · 23 ♒	1 ♏ · 6 ♐	1 ♒ · 19 ♓	1 ♐ · 14 ♑	1 ♒	1 ♑ · 8 ♒	1 ♏ · 3 ♐ · 28 ♑
FEB	1 ♓ · 3 ♈	1 ♒ · 16 ♓	1 ♐ · 7 ♑	1 ♓ · 12 ♈	1 ♑ · 7 ♒	1 ♒	1 ♒ · 3 ♓ · 25 ♈	1 ♑ · 21 ♒
MAR	1 ♈ · 12 ♉	1 ♓ · 12 ♈	1 ♑ · 5 ♒	1 ♈ · 8 ♉	1 ♒ · 3 ♓ · 27 ♈	1 ♒	1 ♈ · 22 ♉	1 ♒ · 17 ♓
APR	1 ♉ · 8 ♈	1 ♈ · 6 ♉ · 30 ♊	1 ♓ · 26 ♈	1 ♉ · 5 ♊	1 ♈ · 20 ♉	1 ♒ · 7 ♓	1 ♉ · 16 ♊	1 ♈ · 10 ♉
MAY	1 ♈	1 ♊ · 25 ♋	1 ♈ · 21 ♉	1 ♊ · 21 ♋	1 ♉ · 15 ♊	1 ♓ · 6 ♈	1 ♊ · 12 ♋	1 ♈ · 5 ♉ · 29 ♊
JUN	1 ♈ · 5 ♉	1 ♋ · 19 ♌	1 ♉ · 14 ♊	1 ♋ · 30 ♊	1 ♊ · 8 ♋	1 ♈ · 2 ♉ · 28 ♊	1 ♋ · 8 ♌	1 ♊ · 23 ♋
JUL	1 ♉ · 8 ♊	1 ♌ · 14 ♍	1 ♊ · 9 ♋	1 ♊	1 ♋ · 2 ♌ · 27 ♍	1 ♊ · 23 ♋	1 ♌ · 9 ♍	1 ♋ · 17 ♌
AUG	1 ♊ · 5 ♋ · 31 ♌	1 ♍ · 10 ♎	1 ♋ · 3 ♌ · 27 ♍	1 ♊ · 4 ♋	1 ♍ · 21 ♎	1 ♌ · 17 ♍	1 ♍	1 ♋ · 10 ♌
SEP	1 ♌ · 25 ♍	1 ♎ · 8 ♏	1 ♍ · 20 ♎	1 ♋ · 9 ♌	1 ♎ · 15 ♏	1 ♌ · 11 ♍	1 ♍	1 ♍ · 4 ♎ · 28 ♏
OCT	1 ♍ · 20 ♎	1 ♏ · 17 ♐	1 ♎ · 14 ♏	1 ♌ · 14 ♍	1 ♏ · 11 ♐	1 ♍ · 5 ♎ · 29 ♏	1 ♍	1 ♏ · 23 ♐
NOV	1 ♎ · 13 ♏	1 ♐ · 9 ♏	1 ♏ · 7 ♐	1 ♍ · 2 ♎ · 27 ♏	1 ♐ · 7 ♑	1 ♏ · 22 ♐	1 ♍ · 10 ♎	1 ♐ · 16 ♑
DEC	1 ♏ · 7 ♐ · 31 ♑	1 ♏	1 ♐ · 2 ♑ · 26 ♒	1 ♏ · 21 ♐	1 ♑ · 7 ♒	1 ♐ · 15 ♑	1 ♎ · 9 ♏	1 ♑ · 11 ♒

– VENUS TABLES –

♀	1953	1954	1955	1956	1957	1958	1959	1960
JAN	1 ♒ 6 ♓	1 ♑ 23 ♒	1 ♏ 7 ♐	1 ♒ 18 ♓	1 ♐ 13 ♑	1 ♒	1 ♑ 8 ♒	1 ♏ 3 ♐ 28 ♑
FEB	1 ♓ 3 ♈	1 ♒ 16 ♓	1 ♐ 7 ♑	1 ♓ 12 ♈	1 ♑ 6 ♒	1 ♒	1 ♓ 25 ♈	1 ♑ 21 ♒
MAR	1 ♈ 15 ♉	1 ♓ 12 ♈	1 ♑ 5 ♒ 31 ♓	1 ♈ 8 ♉	1 ♒ 2 ♓ 26 ♈	1 ♒	1 ♈ 21 ♉	1 ♒ 16 ♓
APR	1 ♈	1 ♈ 5 ♉ 29 ♊	1 ♓ 25 ♈	1 ♉ 5 ♊	1 ♈ 19 ♉	1 ♒	1 ♉ 15 ♊	1 ♓ 10 ♈
MAY	1 ♈	1 ♊ 24 ♋	1 ♈ 20 ♉	1 ♋	1 ♉ 14 ♊	1 ♒ 6 ♓	1 ♊ 11 ♋	1 ♈ 4 ♉ 29 ♊
JUN	1 ♈ 6 ♉	1 ♋ 18 ♌	1 ♉ 14 ♊	1 ♉ 24 ♊	1 ♊ 7 ♋	1 ♓ 2 ♈ 27 ♉	1 ♋ 7 ♌	1 ♊ 22 ♋
JUL	1 ♉ 8 ♊	1 ♌ 14 ♍	1 ♊ 9 ♋	1 ♊	1 ♋ 2 ♌ 27 ♍	1 ♉ 22 ♊	1 ♌ 9 ♍	1 ♋ 16 ♌
AUG	1 ♊ 5 ♋ 31 ♌	1 ♍ 10 ♎	1 ♋ 2 ♌ 26 ♍	1 ♊ 5 ♋	1 ♍ 21 ♎	1 ♋ 16 ♌	1 ♍	1 ♌ 9 ♍
SEP	1 ♌ 25 ♍	1 ♎ 7 ♏	1 ♍ 19 ♎	1 ♋ 9 ♌	1 ♎ 15 ♏	1 ♌ 10 ♍	1 ♍ 21 ♎ 26 ♏	1 ♍ 3 ♎ 28 ♏
OCT	1 ♍ 19 ♎	1 ♏ 24 ♐ 28 ♏	1 ♎ 13 ♏	1 ♌ 7 ♍	1 ♏ 11 ♐	1 ♍ 3 ♎ 28 ♏	1 ♏	1 ♏ 22 ♐
NOV	1 ♎ 12 ♏	1 ♏	1 ♏ 6 ♐	1 ♍ 26 ♎	1 ♐ 6 ♑	1 ♏ 21 ♐	1 ♏ 10 ♐	1 ♐ 16 ♑
DEC	1 ♏ 6 ♐ 30 ♑	1 ♏	1 ♐ 25 ♑	1 ♎ 20 ♏	1 ♑ 7 ♒	1 ♐ 15 ♑	1 ♐ 8 ♑	1 ♑ 11 ♒

♀	1961	1962	1963	1964	1965	1966	1967	1968
JAN	1 ♒ 6 ♓	1 ♑ 22 ♒	1 ♏ 7 ♐	1 ♒ 17 ♓	1 ♐ 13 ♑	1 ♒	1 ♑ 7 ♒ 31 ♓	1 ♏ 2 ♐ 27 ♑
FEB	1 ♓ 3 ♈	1 ♒ 15 ♓	1 ♐ 6 ♑	1 ♓ 11 ♈	1 ♑ 6 ♒	1 ♒ 26 ♑	1 ♓ 24 ♈	1 ♑ 21 ♒
MAR	1 ♈	1 ♓ 11 ♈	1 ♑ 5 ♒ 31 ♓	1 ♈ 8 ♉	1 ♒ 2 ♓ 26 ♈	1 ♒	1 ♈ 21 ♉	1 ♒ 16 ♓
APR	1 ♈	1 ♈ 4 ♉ 29 ♊	1 ♓ 25 ♈	1 ♉ 5 ♊	1 ♈ 19 ♉	1 ♒	1 ♉ 15 ♊	1 ♓ 9 ♈
MAY	1 ♈	1 ♊ 24 ♋	1 ♈ 20 ♉	1 ♉ 10 ♊	1 ♉ 13 ♊	1 ♓ 6 ♈	1 ♊ 11 ♋	1 ♈ 4 ♉ 28 ♊
JUN	1 ♈ 6 ♉	1 ♋ 18 ♌	1 ♉ 13 ♊	1 ♊ 18 ♋	1 ♊ 7 ♋	1 ♈ 27 ♉	1 ♋ 7 ♌	1 ♊ 21 ♋
JUL	1 ♉ 8 ♊	1 ♌ 13 ♍	1 ♊ 8 ♋	1 ♋	1 ♋ 26 ♌	1 ♊ 22 ♋	1 ♌ 9 ♍	1 ♋ 16 ♌
AUG	1 ♊ 4 ♋ 30 ♌	1 ♍ 26 ♎	1 ♋ 6 ♌	1 ♋ 20 ♌	1 ♌ 16 ♍	1 ♋	1 ♍ 10 ♎	1 ♌ 9 ♍
SEP	1 ♌ 24 ♍	1 ♎ 8 ♏	1 ♍ 18 ♎	1 ♌ 9 ♍	1 ♍ 14 ♎	1 ♍	1 ♎ 10 ♏	1 ♍ 3 ♎ 27 ♏
OCT	1 ♍ 18 ♎	1 ♏	1 ♎ 13 ♏	1 ♍ 6 ♎	1 ♎ 10 ♏	1 ♍ 3 ♎ 27 ♏	1 ♏ 2 ♐	1 ♏ 22 ♐
NOV	1 ♎ 12 ♏	1 ♏	1 ♎ 6 ♏ 30 ♐	1 ♎ 25 ♏	1 ♏ 6 ♐	1 ♏ 20 ♐	1 ♐ 10 ♑	1 ♐ 15 ♑
DEC	1 ♏ 6 ♐ 29 ♑	1 ♏	1 ♐ 24 ♑	1 ♐ 20 ♑	1 ♐ 8 ♑	1 ♐ 14 ♑	1 ♐ 8 ♑	1 ♑ 10 ♒

♀	1969	1970	1971	1972	1973	1974	1975	1976
JAN	1 ♒ 5 ♓	1 ♑ 22 ♒	1 ♏ 8 ♐	1 ♒ 17 ♓	1 ♐ 12 ♑	1 ♒ 30 ♑	1 ♑ 7 ♒ 31 ♓	1 ♏ 2 ♐ 27 ♑
FEB	1 ♓ 3 ♈	1 ♒ 15 ♓	1 ♐ 6 ♑	1 ♓ 11 ♈	1 ♑ 5 ♒	1 ♑	1 ♓ 24 ♈	1 ♑ 20 ♒
MAR	1 ♈	1 ♓ 11 ♈	1 ♑ 5 ♒ 30 ♓	1 ♈ 8 ♉	1 ♓ 25 ♈	1 ♒	1 ♈ 20 ♉	1 ♒ 15 ♓
APR	1 ♈	1 ♈ 4 ♉ 28 ♊	1 ♓ 24 ♈	1 ♉ 3 ♊	1 ♈ 19 ♉	1 ♒ 7 ♓	1 ♉ 14 ♊	1 ♓ 9 ♈
MAY	1 ♈	1 ♊ 23 ♋	1 ♈ 19 ♉	1 ♊ 11 ♋	1 ♉ 13 ♊	1 ♓ 5 ♈	1 ♊ 10 ♋	1 ♈ 3 ♉ 27 ♊
JUN	1 ♈ 6 ♉	1 ♋ 17 ♌	1 ♉ 13 ♊	1 ♋ 12 ♊	1 ♊ 6 ♋	1 ♉ 26 ♊	1 ♋ 7 ♌	1 ♊ 21 ♋
JUL	1 ♉ 8 ♊	1 ♌ 13 ♍	1 ♊ 7 ♋	1 ♊	1 ♋ 26 ♌	1 ♊ 22 ♋	1 ♌ 10 ♍	1 ♋ 15 ♌
AUG	1 ♊ 4 ♋ 30 ♌	1 ♍ 9 ♎	1 ♋ 25 ♌	1 ♊ 7 ♋	1 ♌ 19 ♍	1 ♋ 15 ♌	1 ♍	1 ♌ 9 ♍
SEP	1 ♌ 24 ♍	1 ♎ 8 ♏	1 ♍ 18 ♎	1 ♋ 8 ♌	1 ♍ 14 ♎	1 ♌ 9 ♍	1 ♍ 3 ♎	1 ♍ 2 ♎ 26 ♏
OCT	1 ♍ 18 ♎	1 ♏	1 ♎ 12 ♏	1 ♌ 6 ♍ 31 ♎	1 ♏ 10 ♐	1 ♍ 3 ♎ 27 ♏	1 ♌ 5 ♍	1 ♏ 21 ♐
NOV	1 ♎ 11 ♏	1 ♏	1 ♏ 5 ♐ 30 ♑	1 ♎ 25 ♏	1 ♐ 6 ♑	1 ♏ 20 ♐	1 ♍ 10 ♎	1 ♐ 15 ♑
DEC	1 ♏ 5 ♐ 29 ♑	1 ♏	1 ♑ 24 ♒	1 ♏ 19 ♐	1 ♑ 8 ♒	1 ♐ 14 ♑	1 ♎ 7 ♏	1 ♑ 10 ♒

♀	1977	1978	1979	1980	1981	1982	1983	1984
JAN	1 ♒ 5 ♓	1 ♑ 21 ♒	1 ♏ 8 ♐	1 ♒ 16 ♓	1 ♐ 12 ♑	1 ♒ 24 ♑	1 ♑ 6 ♒ 30 ♓	1 ♏ 2 ♐ 26 ♑
FEB	1 ♓ 3 ♈	1 ♒ 14 ♓	1 ♐ 6 ♑	1 ♓ 10 ♈	1 ♑ 5 ♒ 28 ♓	1 ♑	1 ♓ 23 ♈	1 ♑ 20 ♒
MAR	1 ♈	1 ♓ 10 ♈	1 ♑ 4 ♒ 29 ♓	1 ♈ 7 ♉	1 ♓ 25 ♈	1 ♑ 3 ♒	1 ♈ 20 ♉	1 ♒ 15 ♓
APR	1 ♈	1 ♈ 3 ♉ 28 ♊	1 ♓ 23 ♈	1 ♉ 4 ♊	1 ♈ 18 ♉	1 ♒ 7 ♓	1 ♉ 14 ♊	1 ♓ 8 ♈
MAY	1 ♈	1 ♊ 22 ♋	1 ♈ 18 ♉	1 ♊ 13 ♋	1 ♉ 12 ♊	1 ♓ 5 ♈ 31 ♉	1 ♊ 10 ♋	1 ♈ 3 ♉ 27 ♊
JUN	1 ♈ 7 ♉	1 ♋ 17 ♌	1 ♉ 12 ♊	1 ♋ 12 ♊	1 ♊ 6 ♋ 30 ♌	1 ♉ 26 ♊	1 ♋ 7 ♌	1 ♊ 21 ♋
JUL	1 ♉ 7 ♊	1 ♌ 12 ♍	1 ♊ 7 ♋ 31 ♌	1 ♊	1 ♋ 25 ♌	1 ♊ 21 ♋	1 ♌ 11 ♍	1 ♋ 15 ♌
AUG	1 ♊ 3 ♋ 29 ♌	1 ♍ 8 ♎	1 ♋ 25 ♌	1 ♊ 7 ♋	1 ♌ 19 ♍	1 ♋ 15 ♌	1 ♌ 28 ♍	1 ♌ 8 ♍
SEP	1 ♌ 23 ♍	1 ♎ 8 ♏	1 ♍ 18 ♎	1 ♋ 8 ♌	1 ♌ 13 ♍	1 ♌ 8 ♍	1 ♌	1 ♍ 2 ♎ 26 ♏
OCT	1 ♍ 17 ♎	1 ♏	1 ♎ 12 ♏	1 ♌ 5 ♍ 31 ♎	1 ♏ 9 ♐	1 ♍ 2 ♎ 26 ♏	1 ♌ 6 ♍	1 ♏ 21 ♐
NOV	1 ♎ 11 ♏	1 ♏	1 ♏ 5 ♐ 29 ♑	1 ♎ 25 ♏	1 ♐ 6 ♑	1 ♏ 19 ♐	1 ♎ 10 ♏	1 ♐ 14 ♑
DEC	1 ♏ 4 ♐ 28 ♑	1 ♏	1 ♑ 23 ♒	1 ♏ 19 ♐	1 ♑ 9 ♒	1 ♐ 12 ♑	1 ♎ 7 ♏	1 ♑ 10 ♒

♀	1985	1986	1987	1988	1989	1990	1991	1992
JAN	1♒ 5♓	1♑ 21♒	1♏ 8♐	1♒ 16♓	1♐ 11♑	1♒ 17♑	1♑ 6♒ 30♓	1♐ 26♑
FEB	1♓ 3♈	1♒ 14♓	1♐ 6♑	1♓ 10♈	1♑ 4♒ 28♓	1♑	1♓ 23♈	1♑ 19♒
MAR	1♈	1♓ 9♈	1♑ 4♒ 29♓	1♈ 7♉	1♓ 24♈	1♑ 4♒	1♈ 19♉	1♒ 14♓
APR	1♈	1♈ 3♉ 27♊	1♓ 6♈	1♉ 4♊	1♈ 17♉	1♒ 16♓	1♉ 13♊	1♓ 7♈
MAY	1♈	1♊ 22♋	1♈ 18♉	1♊ 18♋ 27♊	1♉ 12♊	1♓ 4♈ 31♉	1♊ 9♋	1♈ 2♉ 26♊
JUN	1♈ 7♉	1♋ 16♌	1♉ 12♊	1♊	1♊ 5♋ 30♌	1♉ 25♊	1♋ 7♌	1♊ 20♋
JUL	1♉ 7♊	1♌ 12♍	1♊ 6♋ 31♌	1♊	1♌ 24♍	1♊ 20♋	1♌ 11♍	1♋ 14♌
AUG	1♊ 3♋ 28♌	1♍ 8♎	1♌ 24♍	1♊ 7♋	1♍ 18♎	1♋ 13♌	1♍ 22♎	1♌ 7♍
SEP	1♌ 23♍	1♎ 8♏	1♍ 17♎	1♋ 8♌	1♎ 13♏	1♌ 9♍	1♌	1♎ 25♏
OCT	1♍ 17♎	1♏	1♎ 11♏	1♌ 5♍ 30♎	1♏ 9♐	1♍ 2♎ 26♏	1♌ 7♍	1♏ 20♐
NOV	1♎ 10♏	1♏	1♏ 4♐ 28♑	1♎ 24♏	1♐ 6♑	1♏ 19♐	1♍ 9♎	1♐ 14♑
DEC	1♏ 4♐ 28♑	1♏	1♑ 23♒	1♏ 18♐	1♑ 10♒	1♐ 13♑	1♎ 7♏	1♑ 9♒

♀	1993	1994	1995	1996	1997	1998	1999	2000
JAN	1♒ 4♓	1♑ 20♒	1♏ 8♐	1♒ 15♓	1♐ 10♑	1♒ 10♑	1♑ 5♒ 29♓	1♐ 25♑
FEB	1♓ 3♈	1♒ 13♓	1♐ 5♑	1♓ 9♈	1♑ 4♒ 28♓	1♑	1♓ 22♈	1♑ 19♒
MAR	1♈	1♓ 9♈	1♑ 3♒ 29♓	1♈ 6♉	1♓ 24♈	1♑ 5♒	1♈ 19♉	1♒ 14♓
APR	1♈	1♈ 2♉ 27♊	1♓ 6♈	1♉ 4♊	1♈ 17♉	1♒ 7♓	1♉ 13♊	1♓ 7♈
MAY	1♈	1♊ 21♋	1♈ 17♉	1♊	1♉ 11♊	1♓ 4♈ 30♉	1♊ 9♋	1♈ 2♉ 26♊
JUN	1♈ 7♉	1♋ 15♌	1♉ 11♊	1♊	1♊ 4♋ 29♌	1♉ 25♊	1♋ 6♌	1♊ 19♋
JUL	1♉ 6♊	1♌ 12♍	1♊ 6♋ 30♌	1♊	1♌ 24♍	1♊ 20♋	1♌ 13♍	1♋ 14♌
AUG	1♊ 2♋ 28♌	1♍ 8♎	1♌ 23♍	1♊ 8♋	1♍ 18♎	1♋ 14♌	1♍ 16♌	1♌ 7♍
SEP	1♌ 22♍	1♎ 8♏	1♍ 17♎	1♋ 8♌	1♎ 12♏	1♌ 7♍	1♌	1♎ 25♏
OCT	1♍ 16♎	1♏	1♎ 11♏	1♌ 5♍ 30♎	1♏ 9♐	1♎ 25♏	1♌ 8♍	1♏ 20♐
NOV	1♎ 9♏	1♏	1♏ 4♐ 28♑	1♎ 24♏	1♐ 6♑	1♏ 18♐	1♍ 10♎	1♐ 13♑
DEC	1♏ 3♐ 27♑	1♏	1♑ 22♒	1♏ 17♐	1♑ 12♒	1♐ 12♑	1♎ 6♏	1♑ 9♒

♂	1921	1922	1923	1924	1925	1926	1927	1928	1929	1930
JAN	1 ♒ 5 ♓	1 ♏	1 ♓ 21 ♈	1 ♏ 19 ♐	1 ♈	1 ♐	1 ♉	1 ♐ 19 ♑	1 ♊	1 ♑
FEB	1 ♓ 13 ♈	1 ♏ 18 ♐	1 ♈	1 ♐	1 ♈ 5 ♉	1 ♐ 9 ♑	1 ♉ 22 ♊	1 ♑ 28 ♒	1 ♊	1 ♑ 6 ♒
MAR	1 ♈ 25 ♉	1 ♐	1 ♈ 4 ♉	1 ♐ 6 ♑	1 ♉ 24 ♊	1 ♑ 23 ♒	1 ♊	1 ♒	1 ♊ 10 ♋	1 ♒ 17 ♓
APR	1 ♉	1 ♐	1 ♉ 16 ♊	1 ♑ 24 ♒	1 ♊	1 ♒	1 ♊ 17 ♋	1 ♒ 7 ♓	1 ♋	1 ♓ 24 ♈
MAY	1 ♉ 6 ♊	1 ♐	1 ♊ 30 ♋	1 ♒	1 ♊ 9 ♋	1 ♒ 3 ♓	1 ♋	1 ♓ 16 ♈	1 ♋ 13 ♌	1 ♈
JUN	1 ♊ 18 ♋	1 ♐	1 ♋	1 ♒ 24 ♓	1 ♋ 26 ♌	1 ♓ 15 ♈	1 ♋ 6 ♌	1 ♈ 26 ♉	1 ♌	1 ♈ 3 ♉
JUL	1 ♋	1 ♐	1 ♋ 16 ♌	1 ♓	1 ♌	1 ♈	1 ♌ 25 ♍	1 ♉	1 ♌ 4 ♍	1 ♉ 14 ♊
AUG	1 ♋ 3 ♌	1 ♐	1 ♌	1 ♓ 24 ♒	1 ♌ 12 ♍	1 ♈ 8 ♉	1 ♍	1 ♉ 9 ♊	1 ♍ 21 ♎	1 ♊ 28 ♋
SEP	1 ♌ 19 ♍	1 ♐ 13 ♑	1 ♍	1 ♒	1 ♍ 28 ♎	1 ♉	1 ♍ 10 ♎	1 ♊	1 ♎	1 ♋
OCT	1 ♍	1 ♑ 30 ♒	1 ♍ 18 ♎	1 ♒ 19 ♓	1 ♎	1 ♉	1 ♎ 26 ♏	1 ♊ 3 ♋	1 ♎ 6 ♏	1 ♋ 20 ♌
NOV	1 ♍ 6 ♎	1 ♒	1 ♎	1 ♓	1 ♎ 13 ♏	1 ♉	1 ♏	1 ♋	1 ♏ 18 ♐	1 ♌
DEC	1 ♎ 26 ♏	1 ♒ 11 ♓	1 ♎ 4 ♏	1 ♓ 19 ♈	1 ♏ 28 ♐	1 ♉	1 ♏ 8 ♐	1 ♋ 20 ♊	1 ♐ 29 ♑	1 ♌

♂	1931	1932	1933	1934	1935	1936	1937	1938	1939	1940
JAN	1 ♌	1 ♑ 18 ♒	1 ♍	1 ♒	1 ♎	1 ♒ 14 ♓	1 ♎ 30 ♏	1 ♓ 30 ♈	1 ♏ 29 ♐	1 ♓ 4 ♈
FEB	1 ♌ 16 ♋	1 ♒ 25 ♓	1 ♍	1 ♒ 4 ♓	1 ♎	1 ♓ 22 ♈	1 ♏	1 ♈	1 ♐	1 ♈ 17 ♉
MAR	1 ♋ 30 ♌	1 ♓	1 ♍	1 ♓ 14 ♈	1 ♎	1 ♈	1 ♏ 13 ♐	1 ♈ 12 ♉	1 ♐ 21 ♑	1 ♉
APR	1 ♌	1 ♓ 3 ♈	1 ♍	1 ♈ 22 ♉	1 ♎	1 ♈ 8 ♉	1 ♐	1 ♉ 23 ♊	1 ♑	1 ♉ 7 ♊
MAY	1 ♌	1 ♈ 12 ♉	1 ♍	1 ♉	1 ♎	1 ♉ 13 ♊	1 ♐ 14 ♏	1 ♊	1 ♑ 25 ♒	1 ♊ 17 ♋
JUN	1 ♌ 10 ♍	1 ♉ 8 ♊	1 ♍	1 ♉ 2 ♊	1 ♎	1 ♊ 25 ♋	1 ♏	1 ♊ 7 ♋	1 ♒	1 ♋
JUL	1 ♍	1 ♊	1 ♍ 6 ♎	1 ♊ 15 ♋	1 ♎ 29 ♏	1 ♋	1 ♏	1 ♋ 22 ♌	1 ♒ 21 ♑	1 ♋ 3 ♌
AUG	1 ♎	1 ♊ 4 ♋	1 ♎ 26 ♏	1 ♋ 30 ♌	1 ♏	1 ♋ 10 ♌	1 ♏ 8 ♐	1 ♌	1 ♑	1 ♌ 19 ♍
SEP	1 ♎ 17 ♏	1 ♋ 20 ♌	1 ♏	1 ♌	1 ♏ 16 ♐	1 ♌ 26 ♍	1 ♐ 30 ♑	1 ♌ 7 ♍	1 ♑ 24 ♒	1 ♍
OCT	1 ♏ 30 ♐	1 ♌	1 ♏ 9 ♐	1 ♌ 18 ♍	1 ♐ 28 ♑	1 ♍	1 ♑	1 ♍ 25 ♎	1 ♒	1 ♍ 5 ♎
NOV	1 ♐	1 ♌ 13 ♍	1 ♐ 19 ♑	1 ♍	1 ♑	1 ♍ 14 ♎	1 ♑ 11 ♒	1 ♎	1 ♒ 19 ♓	1 ♎ 20 ♏
DEC	1 ♐ 10 ♑	1 ♍	1 ♑ 28 ♒	1 ♍ 11 ♎	1 ♑ 7 ♒	1 ♎	1 ♒ 21 ♓	1 ♎ 11 ♏	1 ♓	1 ♏

♂	1941	1942	1943	1944	1945	1946	1947	1948	1949	1950
JAN	1 ♏ 4 ♐	1 ♈ 11 ♉	1 ♐ 26 ♑	1 ♊	1 ♐ 5 ♑	1 ♋	1 ♑ 25 ♒	1 ♍	1 ♑ 4 ♒	1 ♎
FEB	1 ♐ 17 ♑	1 ♉	1 ♑	1 ♊	1 ♑ 14 ♒	1 ♋	1 ♒	1 ♍ 12 ♌	1 ♒ 11 ♓	1 ♎
MAR	1 ♑	1 ♉ 7 ♊	1 ♑ 8 ♒	1 ♊ 29 ♋	1 ♒ 25 ♓	1 ♋	1 ♒ 4 ♓	1 ♌	1 ♓ 21 ♈	1 ♎ 28 ♍
APR	1 ♑ 2 ♒	1 ♊ 26 ♋	1 ♒ 17 ♓	1 ♋	1 ♓	1 ♋ 22 ♌	1 ♓ 11 ♈	1 ♌	1 ♈ 30 ♉	1 ♍
MAY	1 ♒ 16 ♓	1 ♋	1 ♓ 27 ♈	1 ♋ 22 ♌	1 ♓ 3 ♈	1 ♌	1 ♈ 21 ♉	1 ♌ 18 ♍	1 ♉	1 ♍
JUN	1 ♓	1 ♋ 14 ♌	1 ♈	1 ♌	1 ♈ 11 ♉	1 ♌ 20 ♍	1 ♉	1 ♍	1 ♉ 10 ♊	1 ♍ 11 ♎
JUL	1 ♓ 2 ♈	1 ♌	1 ♈ 7 ♉	1 ♌ 12 ♍	1 ♉ 23 ♊	1 ♍	1 ♊	1 ♍ 17 ♎	1 ♊ 23 ♋	1 ♎
AUG	1 ♈	1 ♍	1 ♉ 23 ♊	1 ♍ 29 ♎	1 ♊	1 ♍ 9 ♎	1 ♊ 13 ♋	1 ♎	1 ♋	1 ♎ 10 ♏
SEP	1 ♈	1 ♍ 17 ♎	1 ♊	1 ♎	1 ♊ 7 ♋	1 ♎ 24 ♏	1 ♋	1 ♎ 3 ♏	1 ♋ 7 ♌	1 ♏ 25 ♐
OCT	1 ♈	1 ♎	1 ♊	1 ♎ 13 ♏	1 ♋	1 ♏	1 ♌	1 ♏ 17 ♐	1 ♌ 27 ♍	1 ♐
NOV	1 ♈	1 ♎ 2 ♏	1 ♊	1 ♏ 25 ♐	1 ♋ 11 ♌	1 ♏ 6 ♐	1 ♌	1 ♐ 26 ♑	1 ♍	1 ♐ 6 ♑
DEC	1 ♈	1 ♏ 15 ♐	1 ♊	1 ♐	1 ♌ 26 ♋	1 ♐ 17 ♑	1 ♍	1 ♑	1 ♍ 26 ♎	1 ♑ 15 ♒

♂	1951	1952	1953	1954	1955	1956	1957	1958	1959	1960
JAN	1 ♒ 22 ♓	1 ♎ 20 ♏	1 ♓	1 ♍	1 ♓ 15 ♈	1 ♏ 14 ♐	1 ♈ 28 ♉	1 ♐	1 ♉	1 ♐ 14 ♑
FEB	1 ♓	1 ♏	1 ♓ 8 ♈	1 ♍ 9 ♎	1 ♈ 26 ♉	1 ♐ 28 ♑	1 ♉	1 ♐ 3 ♑	1 ♉ 10 ♊	1 ♑ 23 ♒
MAR	1 ♓ 2 ♈	1 ♏	1 ♈ 20 ♉	1 ♎	1 ♉	1 ♑	1 ♉ 17 ♊	1 ♑ 17 ♒	1 ♊	1 ♒
APR	1 ♈ 10 ♉	1 ♏	1 ♉	1 ♎ 12 ♏	1 ♉ 10 ♊	1 ♑ 14 ♒	1 ♊	1 ♒ 27 ♓	1 ♊ 10 ♋	1 ♒ 2 ♓
MAY	1 ♉ 21 ♊	1 ♏	1 ♉	1 ♏	1 ♊ 26 ♋	1 ♒	1 ♊ 4 ♋	1 ♓	1 ♋	1 ♓ 11 ♈
JUN	1 ♊	1 ♏	1 ♉ 14 ♊	1 ♏	1 ♋	1 ♒ 3 ♓	1 ♋ 21 ♌	1 ♓ 7 ♈	1 ♋ 2 ♌	1 ♈ 20 ♉
JUL	1 ♊ 3 ♋	1 ♏	1 ♊ 29 ♋	1 ♏ 3 ♐	1 ♋ 11 ♌	1 ♓	1 ♌	1 ♈ 21 ♉	1 ♌ 20 ♍	1 ♉
AUG	1 ♋ 18 ♌	1 ♏ 27 ♐	1 ♋	1 ♐ 24 ♑	1 ♌ 27 ♍	1 ♓	1 ♌ 8 ♍	1 ♉	1 ♍	1 ♉ 2 ♊
SEP	1 ♌	1 ♐	1 ♋ 14 ♌	1 ♑	1 ♍	1 ♓	1 ♍ 24 ♎	1 ♉ 21 ♊	1 ♍ 5 ♎	1 ♊ 21 ♋
OCT	1 ♌ 5 ♍	1 ♐ 12 ♑	1 ♌	1 ♑ 21 ♒	1 ♍ 13 ♎	1 ♓	1 ♎	1 ♊ 29 ♉	1 ♎ 21 ♏	1 ♋
NOV	1 ♍ 24 ♎	1 ♑ 21 ♒	1 ♌	1 ♒	1 ♎ 29 ♏	1 ♓	1 ♎ 8 ♏	1 ♉	1 ♏	1 ♋
DEC	1 ♎	1 ♒ 30 ♓	1 ♌ 20 ♍	1 ♒ 4 ♓	1 ♏	1 ♓ 6 ♈	1 ♏ 23 ♐	1 ♉	1 ♏ 3 ♐	1 ♋

– MARS TABLES –

♂	1961	1962	1963	1964	1965	1966	1967	1968	1969	1970
JAN	1 ♋	1 ♑	1 ♌	1 ♑ 13 ♒	1 ♍	1 ♒ 30 ♓	1 ♎	1 ♒ 9 ♓	1 ♏	1 ♓ 24 ♈
FEB	1 ♋ 5 ♊ 7 ♋	1 ♑ 2 ♒	1 ♌	1 ♒ 20 ♓	1 ♓	1 ♓	1 ♎ 12 ♏	1 ♓ 17 ♈	1 ♏ 25 ♐	1 ♈
MAR	1 ♋	1 ♒ 12 ♓	1 ♌	1 ♓ 29 ♈	1 ♍	1 ♓ 9 ♈	1 ♏ 31 ♎	1 ♈ 28 ♉	1 ♐	1 ♈ 7 ♉
APR	1 ♋	1 ♓ 19 ♈	1 ♌	1 ♈	1 ♍	1 ♈ 17 ♉	1 ♎	1 ♉	1 ♐	1 ♉ 18 ♊
MAY	1 ♋ 6 ♌	1 ♈ 28 ♉	1 ♌	1 ♈ 7 ♉	1 ♍	1 ♉ 28 ♊	1 ♎	1 ♉ 8 ♊	1 ♐	1 ♊
JUN	1 ♌ 28 ♍	1 ♉	1 ♌ 3 ♍	1 ♉ 17 ♊	1 ♍ 29 ♎	1 ♊	1 ♎	1 ♊ 21 ♋	1 ♐	1 ♊ 2 ♋
JUL	1 ♍	1 ♉ 9 ♊	1 ♍ 27 ♎	1 ♊ 30 ♋	1 ♎	1 ♊ 11 ♋	1 ♎ 19 ♏	1 ♋	1 ♐	1 ♋ 18 ♌
AUG	1 ♍ 17 ♎	1 ♊ 22 ♋	1 ♎	1 ♋	1 ♎ 20 ♏	1 ♋ 25 ♌	1 ♏	1 ♋ 5 ♌	1 ♐	1 ♌
SEP	1 ♎	1 ♋	1 ♎ 12 ♏	1 ♋ 15 ♌	1 ♏	1 ♌	1 ♏ 10 ♐	1 ♌ 21 ♍	1 ♐ 21 ♑	1 ♌ 3 ♍
OCT	1 ♎ 2 ♏	1 ♋ 11 ♌	1 ♏ 25 ♐	1 ♌	1 ♏ 4 ♐	1 ♌ 12 ♍	1 ♐ 23 ♑	1 ♍	1 ♑	1 ♍ 20 ♎
NOV	1 ♏ 13 ♐	1 ♌	1 ♐	1 ♌ 6 ♍	1 ♐ 14 ♑	1 ♍	1 ♑	1 ♍ 9 ♎	1 ♑ 4 ♒	1 ♎
DEC	1 ♐ 24 ♑	1 ♌	1 ♐ 5 ♑	1 ♍	1 ♑ 23 ♒	1 ♍ 4 ♎	1 ♑ 2 ♒	1 ♎ 30 ♏	1 ♒ 15 ♓	1 ♎ 6 ♏

♂	1971	1972	1973	1974	1975	1976	1977	1978	1979	1980
JAN	1 ♏ ♐	1 ♈	1 ♐	1 ♉	1 ♐ 21 ♑	1 ♊	1 ♑	1 ♌ 26 ♋	1 ♑ 21 ♒	1 ♍
FEB	1 ♐	1 ♈ 10 ♉	1 ♐ 12 ♑	1 ♉ 27 ♊	1 ♑	1 ♊	1 ♑ 9 ♒	1 ♋	1 ♒ 28 ♓	1 ♍
MAR	1 ♐ 12 ♑	1 ♉ 27 ♊	1 ♑ 27 ♒	1 ♊	1 ♑ 3 ♒	1 ♊ 18 ♋	1 ♒ 20 ♓	1 ♋	1 ♓	1 ♍ 12 ♌
APR	1 ♑	1 ♊	1 ♒	1 ♊ 20 ♋	1 ♒ 11 ♓	1 ♋	1 ♓ 28 ♈	1 ♋ 11 ♌	1 ♓ 7 ♈	1 ♌
MAY	1 ♑ 3 ♒	1 ♊ 12 ♋	1 ♒ 8 ♓	1 ♋	1 ♓ 21 ♈	1 ♋ 16 ♌	1 ♈	1 ♌	1 ♈ 16 ♉	1 ♌ 4 ♍
JUN	1 ♒	1 ♋ 28 ♌	1 ♓ 21 ♈	1 ♋ 9 ♌	1 ♈	1 ♌	1 ♈ 6 ♉	1 ♌ 14 ♍	1 ♉ 26 ♊	1 ♍
JUL	1 ♒	1 ♌	1 ♈	1 ♌ 27 ♍	1 ♉	1 ♌ 7 ♍	1 ♉ 18 ♊	1 ♍	1 ♊	1 ♍ 11 ♎
AUG	1 ♒	1 ♌ 15 ♍	1 ♈ 12 ♉	1 ♍	1 ♉ 14 ♊	1 ♍ 24 ♎	1 ♊	1 ♍ 4 ♎	1 ♊ 8 ♋	1 ♎ 29 ♏
SEP	1 ♒	1 ♍	1 ♉	1 ♍ 12 ♎	1 ♊	1 ♎	1 ♋	1 ♎ 20 ♏	1 ♋ 25 ♌	1 ♏
OCT	1 ♒	1 ♎	1 ♉ 30 ♈	1 ♎ 28 ♏	1 ♊ 17 ♋	1 ♎ 9 ♏	1 ♋ 27 ♌	1 ♍	1 ♌	1 ♏ 12 ♐
NOV	1 ♒ 6 ♓	1 ♎ 15 ♏	1 ♈	1 ♏	1 ♋ 26 ♊	1 ♏ 21 ♐	1 ♌	1 ♍ 2 ♎	1 ♌ 20 ♍	1 ♐ 22 ♑
DEC	1 ♓ 26 ♈	1 ♏ 30 ♐	1 ♈ 24 ♉	1 ♏ 11 ♐	1 ♊	1 ♐	1 ♌	1 ♐ 13 ♑	1 ♍	1 ♑ 31 ♒

♂	1981	1982	1983	1984	1985	1986	1987	1988	1989	1990
JAN	1 ♒	1 ♎	1 ♒ 17 ♓	1 ♎ 11 ♏	1 ♓	1 ♏	1 ♓ 8 ♈	1 ♏ 9 ♐	1 ♈ 19 ♉	1 ♐ 30 ♑
FEB	1 ♒ 7 ♓	1 ♎	1 ♓ 25 ♈	1 ♏	1 ♓ 3 ♈	1 ♏ 2 ♐	1 ♈ 21 ♉	1 ♐ 22 ♑	1 ♉	1 ♑
MAR	1 ♓ 17 ♈	1 ♎	1 ♈	1 ♏	1 ♈ 15 ♉	1 ♐ 28 ♑	1 ♉	1 ♑	1 ♉ 11 ♊	1 ♑ 12 ♒
APR	1 ♈ 25 ♉	1 ♎	1 ♈ 5 ♉	1 ♏	1 ♉ 26 ♊	1 ♑	1 ♉ 6 ♊	1 ♑ 7 ♒	1 ♊ 29 ♋	1 ♒ 21 ♓
MAY	1 ♉	1 ♎	1 ♉ 17 ♊	1 ♏	1 ♊	1 ♑	1 ♊ 21 ♋	1 ♒ 22 ♓	1 ♋	1 ♓ 31 ♈
JUN	1 ♉ 5 ♊	1 ♎	1 ♊ 29 ♋	1 ♏	1 ♊ 9 ♋	1 ♑	1 ♋	1 ♓	1 ♋ 17 ♌	1 ♈
JUL	1 ♊ 18 ♋	1 ♎	1 ♋	1 ♏	1 ♋ 25 ♌	1 ♑	1 ♋ 7 ♌	1 ♓ 14 ♈	1 ♌	1 ♈ 12 ♉
AUG	1 ♋	1 ♎ 3 ♏	1 ♋ 14 ♌	1 ♏ 18 ♐	1 ♌	1 ♑	1 ♌ 23 ♍	1 ♈	1 ♌ 3 ♍	1 ♉ 31 ♊
SEP	1 ♋ 2 ♌	1 ♏ 20 ♐	1 ♌ 30 ♍	1 ♐	1 ♌ 10 ♍	1 ♑	1 ♍	1 ♈	1 ♍ 20 ♎	1 ♊
OCT	1 ♌ 21 ♍	1 ♐	1 ♍	1 ♐ 5 ♑	1 ♍ 28 ♎	1 ♑ 9 ♒	1 ♍ 9 ♎	1 ♈ 23 ♓	1 ♎	1 ♊
NOV	1 ♍	1 ♑	1 ♍ 18 ♎	1 ♑ 16 ♒	1 ♎	1 ♒ 26 ♓	1 ♎ 24 ♏	1 ♓ 2 ♈	1 ♎ 4 ♏	1 ♊
DEC	1 ♍ 16 ♎	1 ♑ 10 ♒	1 ♎	1 ♒ 25 ♓	1 ♎ 15 ♏	1 ♓	1 ♏	1 ♈	1 ♏ 18 ♐	1 ♊ 14 ♉

♂	1991	1992	1993	1994	1995	1996	1997	1998	1999	2000
JAN	1 ♉ 21 ♊	1 ♐ 9 ♑	1 ♋	1 ♑ 28 ♒	1 ♍ 23 ♌	1 ♑ 8 ♒	1 ♍ 3 ♎	1 ♒ 25 ♓	1 ♎ 26 ♏	1 ♒ 4 ♓
FEB	1 ♊	1 ♑ 18 ♒	1 ♋	1 ♒	1 ♌	1 ♒ 15 ♓	1 ♎	1 ♓	1 ♏	1 ♓ 12 ♈
MAR	1 ♊	1 ♒ 28 ♓	1 ♋	1 ♒ 7 ♓	1 ♌	1 ♓ 24 ♈	1 ♎ 8 ♍	1 ♓ 5 ♈	1 ♏	1 ♈ 23 ♉
APR	1 ♊ 3 ♋	1 ♓	1 ♋ 28 ♌	1 ♓ 15 ♈	1 ♌	1 ♈	1 ♍	1 ♈ 13 ♉	1 ♏	1 ♉
MAY	1 ♋ 27 ♌	1 ♓ 6 ♈	1 ♌	1 ♈ 24 ♉	1 ♌ 26 ♍	1 ♈ 2 ♉	1 ♍	1 ♉ 24 ♊	1 ♏ 6 ♎	1 ♉ 4 ♊
JUN	1 ♌	1 ♈ 15 ♉	1 ♌ 23 ♍	1 ♉	1 ♍	1 ♉ 12 ♊	1 ♍ 19 ♎	1 ♊	1 ♎	1 ♊ 16 ♋
JUL	1 ♌ 16 ♍	1 ♉ 27 ♊	1 ♍	1 ♉ 4 ♊	1 ♍ 21 ♎	1 ♊ 25 ♋	1 ♎	1 ♊ 6 ♋	1 ♎ 5 ♏	1 ♋
AUG	1 ♍	1 ♊	1 ♍ 12 ♎	1 ♊ 17 ♋	1 ♎	1 ♋	1 ♎ 14 ♏	1 ♋ 21 ♌	1 ♏	1 ♌
SEP	1 ♎	1 ♊ 12 ♋	1 ♎ 27 ♏	1 ♋	1 ♎ 7 ♏	1 ♋ 9 ♌	1 ♏ 28 ♐	1 ♌	1 ♏ 3 ♐	1 ♌ 17 ♍
OCT	1 ♎ 17 ♏	1 ♋	1 ♏	1 ♋ 5 ♌	1 ♏ 21 ♐	1 ♌ 30 ♍	1 ♐	1 ♌ 7 ♍	1 ♐ 17 ♑	1 ♍
NOV	1 ♏ 29 ♐	1 ♋	1 ♏ 9 ♐	1 ♌	1 ♐ 30 ♑	1 ♍	1 ♐ 9 ♑	1 ♍ 27 ♎	1 ♑ 26 ♒	1 ♍ 4 ♎
DEC	1 ♐	1 ♋	1 ♐ 20 ♑	1 ♌ 12 ♍	1 ♑	1 ♍	1 ♑ 18 ♒	1 ♎	1 ♒	1 ♎ 23 ♏